IMAGES
of England

ALTON
AND ITS VILLAGES

IMAGES
of England

ALTON
AND ITS VILLAGES

Tony Cross, Jane Hurst
and Martin Morris

TEMPUS

The rural nature of the area around Alton is captured by this image taken during hay making around 100 years ago. Mechanisation came late to many of the small farms in the surrounding villages.

Frontispiece: Map of the Alton area by C. and J. Greenwood, 1826.

First published 2002

Tempus Publishing Limited
The Mill, Brimscombe Port,
Stroud, Gloucestershire, GL5 2QG

British Library Cataloguing in Publication Data.
A catalogue record for this book is available from the British Library.

ISBN 0 7524 2492 0

Typesetting and origination by Tempus Publishing Limited
Printed in Great Britain by Midway Colour Print, Wiltshire

Contents

Introduction

Since the publication of the last *Alton* book in 1999, numerous people have enquired if there was to be a sequel that included local villages. While we have been fortunate to see a range of titles published in recent years covering individual villages, there does not seem to have been one of general local appeal since the publication in 1906, by William Curtis, of *Alton and the Surrounding Villages*.

If you agree with the maxim that two heads are better than one, hopefully you follow the logic that suggests, therefore, three heads are better than two. Accordingly, the three authors, who oversee the production of the popular local history journal *Alton Papers*, embarked on the selection of images and the preparation of captions for this volume that covers Alton and the villages.

In our own researches we use the wealth of material contained in trade directories. These became abundant in the early nineteenth century and were produced on a regular basis until the mid-twentieth century. Their entries include 'potted histories' of individual towns and villages and we have chosen to edit and include those from the 1895 *Kelly's Directory of Hampshire* as an introduction to this book. Many of the pictures featured here date from around this late Victorian period and can therefore be viewed in the context of the information below.

'Alton is a market, union and county court town, parish and railway station on the Farnham and Winchester branch of the London and South Western Railway, 47 miles from London by road and rail. The River Wey rises close to the town. The Local Government Act of 1858 was adopted here 28 August 1860 and the town was governed by a local board until, under the provisions of the Local Government Act of 1894, an Urban District Council was formed. The church of St Lawrence is an ancient and spacious edifice of stone, supported by lofty columns of the Perpendicular style and has a double nave; from the centre of the church on the south side rises a Norman tower which is surmounted by a spire. The church was restored in 1867 at a cost of about £3,600 and there are about 800 seats.

The church of All Saints, on the Winchester road, is a stone building erected in 1874, from designs by Mr F.C. Dyer, architect, London, at a cost of about £3,500 raised by subscription and has seats for 400. In 1881 a square tower and spire were erected with one bell; in 1885 a clock and another bell were added, at a cost of £190. The church registers date from 1875. A cemetery of 3 acres, at the north end of the town, was formed in 1854 at a cost of £1,200.

The town hall was built by subscription in 1813. It is a square brick building, the lower portion being used by corn merchants; the upper floor is a spacious room adapted for balls and assemblies. A market for corn is held every Tuesday and one for cattle and sheep every alternate Tuesday; a considerable lamb market is held on the Butts, near the town, the day after Stockbridge Fair, in July. The annual fairs are on the last Saturday in April (for sheep and cattle) and the 29th of September (for horses, sheep and occasionally hops).

A fire brigade was established in 1863, consisting of the leading tradesmen of the town who have two fire engines, one of which has steam power. The H Company of 1st Volunteer

Battalion Hants Regiment meet at the town hall. Here are two breweries, a paper manufactory, iron foundry and a private lunatic asylum. The Cottage Hospital, established in 1869, was found insufficient for the demands made on it, and a new one providing 8 beds was opened in 1880 at a cost of £2,231.

Thedden Grange, the seat of John Gathorne Wood JP is 2½ miles west of Alton, the grounds are extensive and beautifully wooded. Near it a chapel of ease was built in 1854 with seats for 90, at the expense of the late John Wood. Montagu George Knight of Chawton is lord of the manor of Alton Eastbrook and Henry John Dutton of Alton Westbrook. The principal landowners are Montagu G. Knight, John Gathorne Wood and Winchester College. The soil is clay; subsoil, chalk. The chief crops are corn and hops. The area is 3,925 acres; rateable value, £19,507; the population in 1891 was 4,761 including 7 officers and 116 inmates in the workhouse.

Anstey is a tithing of the parish, about 1 mile north-east. Henry Hall is lord of the manor of Anstey.

Bentworth is 4 miles west from Alton. Bentworth Hall is the seat of the Hon. Mrs Ives, who is lady of the manor. Bentworth Lodge, one mile east, is the residence of Captain Frederick Stephens JP. The principal landowners are Arthur Frederick Jeffreys MP DL JP; Captain Frederick Stephens JP; the Hon. Mrs Ives, Colonel Gordon Ives and John Gathorne Wood JP. The soil is clay; subsoil chalk. The chief crops are wheat, oats and turnips. The area is 3,763 acres; rateable value, £3,298; the population in 1891 was 604.

Burkham is a hamlet 2 miles north of the church. Wivelrod (or Wivelet) is a hamlet, 1½ miles south-east.

Wield is 3½ miles north-west of Medstead station. Here is a Primitive Methodist chapel, built in 1884. The principal landowners are the Earl of Portsmouth and Barnes Wimbush who is lord of the manor. The soil is principally clay; subsoil, clay. The chief crops are wheat, oats and turnips. The area is 2,104 acres; rateable value, £1,245; and the population in 1891 was 234.

Lasham is 4½ miles north-west of Alton. Francis Michael Ellis Jervoise of Herriard Park is lord of the manor and principal landowner. The soil is clay; subsoil, chalk. The chief crops are wheat, oats and turnips. The area is 1,797 acres; rateable value, £1,150; the population in 1891 was 169.

Shalden is 2¾ miles north-west of Alton. John Gathorne Wood of Shalden Manor, is the lord of the manor and principal landowner. The soil is clay and chalk; subsoil, chalk. The chief crops are cereal. The area is 1,535 acres; rateable value, £1,085; the population in 1891 was 175.

Holybourne is a mile to the north west of Alton and the River Wey runs through the parish. Here is a Weslyan chapel built in 1867 and a Presbyterian chapel of 1864. Sir Charles Miller, who is lord of the manor, and John Complin are the principal landowners. The soil is clay; subsoil, chalk. The chief crops are corn and hops. The acreage is 1,405; ratable value, £2,693 and the population in 1891 was 587.

Neatham is a tithing half a mile east of Holybourne on the south side of the Wey. It contains two farmhouses and a few scattered cottages. The area is 1,117 acres; ratable value, £1,267 and the population in 1891 was 102.

Froyle (Upper and Lower) form a parish 3 miles north-east from Alton, 3 miles west of Bentley. The river Wey runs through the parish. The iron church of St Joseph is served by the clergy of St Mary's. There is a Wesleyan chapel, erected in 1862, at Lower Froyle. The principal landowners are Sir C.J. Hubert Miller (who is lord of the manor) and Henry Burningham. The soil is clay; subsoil, chalk and clay. The chief crops are hops and cereals. The area is 3,665 acres; rateable value, £3,548; the population in 1891 was 729.

Three children of this parish are entitled to be educated at the Endowed Free school, Holybourne.

Bentley is on the Alton branch of the South Western Railway, 42 miles from London, 5 miles north-east from Alton. Here is a Bible Christian chapel. The Ecclesiastical Commissioners are lords of the manor. The principal landowners are F.T. Giles, W. Rowcliffe, T.A. Seawell, Mrs Eggar and Mr White. The soil is clay, gravel and chalk marl. The chief crops are corn and hops. The area is 2,299 acres; rateable value, £4,467; the population in 1891 was 727.

Binsted is 4 miles north-east of Alton and 2 miles south-west of Bentley. There are Primitive Methodist, Unsectarian and Wesleyan chapels here. Binsted is entitled to send five children to the school at Holybourne. Binsted-Wyck is the seat of William Wickham MP, DL, JP. The Crown is lord of the manor. The principal landowners are Henry John Dutton, Revd Augustus Legge, Edward Cobden, William Wickham MP, George Langrish and Mrs Ellen Wheeler. The soil is malm; subsoil, gravel. The chief crops are corn and hops. The area is 6,901 acres of land and 19 of water; rateable value, £9,034; the population in 1891 was 1,331, including part of Rowledge.

Isington is a hamlet 1 mile north on the river Wey; Wyck, a hamlet 1 mile south-west; Wheatley, a hamlet 1 mile south-east; Blacknest, 1 mile east; Alice Holt Wood is a large wood to the east; South-Hay, 1 mile south. Bucks Horn Oak is a hamlet in Alice Holt Forest, 2 miles to the north-east.

East Worldham is 2 miles east of Alton. The Wesleyans have a chapel here. Here is a reading room, built in 1893, by John Baigent at his own cost. King John's Hill is reputed to have been the hunting seat of that monarch. The principal landowners are Henry John Dutton who is lord of the manor, William Wickham MP, Montagu George Knight, John Baigent and the governing body of Winchester College. The soil is malm and clay; subsoil, rock. The chief crops are cereals, and some hops are grown. The area is 1,800 acres; rateable value, £1,890; the population in 1891 was 252.

West Worldham is a small village 2½ miles south-east of Alton. Henry John Dutton is the lord of the manor and principal landowner. The soil is loam; subsoil, malm and greensand formation. The chief crops are cereals and hops. The area is 471 acres; rateable value, £527; the population in 1891 was 60. Milkwell is half a mile east.

Hartley Mauditt is 2¾ miles south-east of Alton. Henry John Dutton is lord of the manor and principal landowner. The soil is malm; subsoil, upper greensand. The chief crops are corn and hops. The area is 1,404 acres; rateable value, £1,311; the population in 1891 was 90.

Kingsley is 5 miles south of Bentley. The river Slea flows through the parish. Here is a Congregational chapel. Henry John Dutton is lord of the manor. The principal landowners are Henry John Dutton, William Wickham MP and H. Burningham. The soil is light loam; subsoil, sand. The chief crops are wheat, barley and hops. The area is 1,801 acres; rateable value, £2,207; the population in 1891 was 399.

Selborne is 4½ miles south of Alton. Here is a Congregational chapel. A great portion of Woolmer Forest is in the parish. At the time of the Domesday survey Selborne was held by the Crown. The President and Fellows of Magdalen College, Oxford, are lords of the manor and, with Henry John Dutton, who is lord of the manor of Oakhanger and the Earl of Selborne, are the principal landowners. The soil within the parish is, in succession from the summit level of the hills westward to Woolmer Forest eastward, chalk; black and white malm, with rock of the upper greensand formation below; gault clay; and lower greensand. The chief crops are wheat, barley and hops. The area, including Blackmoor, is 7,819 acres of land and 97 of water; rateable value, £6,144; the population in 1891 was 1,320 including 707 in Blackmoor.

Newton Valence is a 5½ miles south of Alton. Captain Edward Hoare Chawner is the lord of the manor and principal landowner. The soil is clay and chalk; subsoil, gravel and clay. The chief crops are wheat, oats and barley. The area is 2,258 acres; rateable value, £2,122; the population in 1891 was 291.

East Tisted is 4 miles south-west of Alton. Almshouses for three aged couples were erected in 1879 by members of the Scott family; another two were added in 1893. The trustees of the late G.A. Jervoise Scott (died 1895) are lords of the manor and the principal landowners. The soil is clay; chalk subsoil, gravel in the valleys. The chief crops are wheat, oats and barley. The area is 2,648 acres; rateable value, £2,167; the population in 1891 was 184.

Farringdon, or Faringdon, is 3 miles south of Alton. Here is a Wesleyan chapel and a village club and reading rooms. Montagu George Knight JP is lord of the manor and principal landowner. The soil is clay; subsoil, chalk and gravel. The chief crops are corn and hops; the area is 2,357 acres; rateable value, £2,525; the population in 1891 was 517.

Chawton is 1½ miles south-west of Alton. One of the sources of the river Wey is in the parish. The village is in a valley watered by land springs, called Lavants, which occasionally overflow the adjacent lands. Here is a working men's club, which is well supplied with newspapers. M.G. Knight is lord of the manor and principal landowner. The soil is marl; subsoil, gravel and chalk. The chief crops are wheat, oats, barley and hops. Area, 2,674 acres, rateable value £2,857; the population in 1891 was 455.

Medstead has a station, 2 miles south of the village, on the London and South Western Railway, 4 miles south-west from Alton. It is 697 feet above the sea level; there are several ancient wells, but owing to their immense depth they are seldom used, many of the inhabitants being supplied with water from an underground tank which receives the rain from the church and school roofs; most of the houses have now their own tanks and all new houses must be so provided. Here is a Congregational chapel. A cemetery of three-quarters of an acre was formed in 1884 at a cost of £150.

Here is a village hall, consisting of two rooms erected through the kindness of Thomas Miller, late of this parish, for the benefit of the young men; lectures and entertainments are given in it through the winter months; coffee and refreshments are provided by a cheap rate, and games and daily papers supplied. The Ecclesiastical Commissioners are lords of the manor. The principal landowners are Colonel Halliday RA, the trustees of the late William Blackmore, the trustees of the late William Higgs and Messrs C.W. Curtis, J. Cole and Mrs Wake and John Curtis. Boyne's Wood is that part of the parish near Medstead station. The soil is chalk and clay; subsoil, chalk. The chief crops are wheat and oats. The area is 2,848 acres; rateable value, £2,334, the population in 1891 was 451.'

Acknowledgements

The illustrations in this book are taken from the photographic collections of the Hampshire County Council Museums Service, supplemented by images from a number of private collections. The former have been collected by museum staff or donated by the good people of Alton and the surrounding area since the formation of the Curtis Museum almost 150 years ago. The latter have been found more recently at many postcard shows and fairs over a very wide area.

Our thanks are due to numerous people, including the staff at the Rural Life Centre in Tilford who have helped in the preparation of this volume by providing valuable pieces of information, and those who have lent illustrations for our use here. The never-ending support and encouragement of the staff of the Hampshire Record Office and the Hampshire Local Studies Library have aided the research into the local history of the area, aspects of which will be found within these pages.

Finally, the staff of the County Museums Service are to be thanked for their support in this project in many ways – yet another of the well meaning, but time consuming, schemes of a local curator.

Both local and family history have enjoyed considerable popularity over the past thirty years and we hope this book provides further encouragement for local research in the Alton area.

One
Alton, Beech and Thedden

It is fascinating to see the narrow nature of Church Street from its junction with the High Street. The Crown Hotel on the left, the White House in the distance and Geales Almshouses are still there, but the six cottages on the right and the corner shop were demolished forty years ago to make access easier for motor vehicles.

The High Street of today appears little different from this image. 27 High Street, with a large packing case outside, was formerly known as London House. Here it was the shop of Charles Bond, draper, outfitter and boot warehouseman. Fifty years later it was still a general drapers, selling St Margaret and Maid of Kent underwear.

Having become the bakery of William Doggrell by 1852, the corner site on Lenten Street and the Market Place was acquired for £525 on 20 August 1888 by Henry Adlam. With his death it changed hands several times before being taken over by the Buck family in September 1963. They operated a popular bakery until Easter 1991.

Debenham's cycle shop, on the far left, was subject to a planning application by Mr A.J. Martin early in 1914. However the First World War intervened and the shop had been demolished by mid-1919. Until 1878 the Market Hotel was known as the Butcher's Arms. Ten years later, Samuel Henry Lewis advertised his livery and bait stables here.

In the background of the poultry cages, to the left of the Market Hotel, can be seen part of the old Auction Mart. A former First World War Army hut, temporary building permission for it was sought in 1920. The auctions that took place there served a much needed role in the market and the building was only demolished in 2000.

The Salvation Army barracks on the left opened on 4 September 1891. The Alton Corps started on 13 January 1884 and originally met in nearby cottages. The building with the sign on the right was demolished in 1936, while the brick buildings beyond were replaced by three town houses in 1978.

The Scouts and Cubs of the 6th Alton Salvation Army pack dedicated their colours at the Salvation Army Citadel on Sunday 13 September 1959. The ceremony was conducted by Major Parker, the National Scout Organiser of the Salvation Army. C.W. Hawkins, well-known Altonian and a scout master, is third from the right in the back row.

14

The Salvation Army barracks of 1891 became too small and after the Second World War efforts were made to raise funds for a new building. After the meeting on 27 January 1957 the premises were demolished and this new building opened on Saturday 4 January 1958.

This building in Amery Street was formerly the Leather Bottle public house. It closed in 1907 with compensation of £780. Seen here are members of the Friends of the Curtis Museum enjoying an evening visit. The Friends were founded in 1934 to help support the Curtis Museum – a function they are still proud to perform almost seventy years later.

The land on which Brook Cottage stands, seen here with its Coronation decorations of 1953, was bought by William Edwards. He built these two cottages before his death in 1834 and by 1870 buildings had been erected on the Tanhouse Lane end of the property. Originally they were used as workshops and stores by the Wey Iron Works.

About 150 years ago Moses Fielder had a brewery on the site to the left of the picture. When Moses' grandson, Alfred, went bankrupt in 1847 it was said to consist of 'a newly erected brewery fitted up in the first style and a malthouse capable of wetting 18 quarters'. The business was bought by J & J Knight, brewers of Farnham.

The Wey Iron Works was started in 1865 by Messrs Hetherington. A sales catalogue in the Curtis Museum details them as Engineers, Brass and Iron Founders, Agricultural Implement Makers, Wagon, Van and Cart Builders. The entrance seen here is now glazed, forming the end wall of the café in the Community Centre.

Alfred Hetherington was the first Superintendent of the Volunteer Fire Brigade, founded on 15 June 1863. By the time this group was photographed the Chief Officer was William Bradley Trimmer (third from left in flat hat) who retired in 1942 after thirty-one years in the post. He was a local solicitor and the town clerk.

The Manor House in the High Street was built around 1842 by Henry Hall who had come to Alton from Ely, Cambridgeshire, to take over Hawkins' brewery. The house had a large park at the rear with stables, gardens and glass houses. The spire in the background is on top of the old Inwood Hospital, now Inwood Court, in Crown Close.

The right-hand portion of the George Inn was demolished in the mid-nineteenth century while the remainder continued to be used by local businesses. Mr Crow, upholster, cabinet maker and home furnisher, used the old carriage arch to take items through to the buildings behind, one of which dates from 1501 and still lies alongside the river.

The staff of the outfitters shop of Thomas Chesterfield, 42-44 High Street, were keen to decorate their premises for royal events. They put on a good show for the Silver Jubilee of 1935 and again two years later for the Coronation of King George VI on 12 May 1937, seen here. Thomas, who opened his shop in 1877, was the pastor of the Baptist chapel.

In 1828 Alexander Sayer's wagons were leaving his warehouse in Church Street for London every Tuesday and Friday. The business then moved here in Cross and Pillory Lane. By 1911 they were known as Sayers and Cox Ltd, carriers, furniture removers and coal merchants of Market Place, Normandy Street and the Railway Station.

The workmen of J.H. & E. Dyer are seen here putting up lightning conductors after the steeple of St Lawrence's had been struck on 24 June 1880. The firm were widely known throughout Hampshire and there was hardly a church in the northern part of the county that was not built, re-built or renovated by them.

In the late 1800s and early 1900s, this house in Church Street was occupied by Miss Isabell Cooper and her niece Jessie who were both dress makers. Fifty years before, William Rendell opened his Classical Mathematical and Commercial Academy here. He advertised that the health, morals and happiness of the pupils were to be assiduously promoted.

Legislation in 1876 established the principle that all children should receive elementary education. The National School, pictured here, had been built in 1840 for 450 children at a cost of £1,396. Fees were introduced in 1877, but withdrawn in 1891 when elementary education was made free.

With sections for infants, girls and boys the National School amalgamated with the British School in Normandy Street in 1925. St Lawrence's School took the boys and Normandy Street took the girls. In 1939 both became junior schools with older children then going to the new secondary school on Amery Hill.

When the nine year olds of St Lawrence's School were being photographed here, past pupils of the school were also active. This resulted in a reunion that took place on 28 September 1968. A list of the names of class 3 of 1967, supplied by Sally Trimming (now Fury) sitting in the centre row, can be seen in the Curtis Museum.

The Friends Meeting House in Church Street seems to have been in use since 1672, the date set into the boundary wall. The Meeting House closed in 1914 following the death of Miss Louisa Curtis, who was the last to attend. It was re-opened in 1932 by a younger generation and still functions today.

The first mechanical vehicle purchased by Courage & Co. for the Alton brewery was the steam Foden, right, bought in 1916 for £673. In 1920 they acquired their first motor vehicle and seen here are two Basingstoke-made Thornycroft J type lorries, the one on the left being ex-War Department. The registrations on these vehicles appear to date from 1921.

James Baverstock and his father, Thomas, built a brew house in Turk Street in 1763. Eventually James retired to Southampton where he died in December 1815 and his son, James Hinton Baverstock, became bankrupt in 1821. Following this advertisement, the brewery was sold to A.C.S. & H. Crowley, brewers of Croydon.

a Plan *of the Estate and a Drawing of the House may be seen.*

ALTON, HANTS.

Capital FREEHOLD BREWERY,
WITH SEVERAL PUBLIC HOUSES,
IN THE TOWN AND NEIGHBOURHOOD,
Together with a superior Residence and Offices,
A little Removed from the Brewery,
FOR PEREMPTORY SALE,
By Messrs. ROBINS,
At the Auction Mart, on Thursday, May 24, at twelve,
by direction of the Assignees,

A Valuable FREEHOLD ESTATE, comprehending that Old-established and highly respectable Property,

THE ALTON BREWERY,

justly famed for very many years, for the peculiar quality and superior excellence of its Ale. The Brewery has been planted and completed in the best manner, and possesses every requisite to conduct it prosperously. The Trade, which during the war was 13,000 Barrels, it is known that by encreasing the Capital, it may be materially improved. The Public Houses attached to the Property, and the Free Trade, include Houses of a superior class, and the Private Trade is very considerable. The Residence in front of the High Mail Road, is entirely suited to the occupation of a Gentleman.

The whole is presented as an opportunity very favourable for investment. May be viewed by application at the Alton Brewery.

Printed particulars are ready for delivery at the Office of Mr. John Ellis, Southampton Buildings; Messrs. Amory and Coles, 25, Throgmorton-street; Mr. R. S. Taylor, Field Court, Gray's Inn; Mr. Clement, Alton, Hants; the Auction Mart, and in Covent Garden.

TO BE SOLD BY AUCTION,
By Mr. FAULKNOR,

On Friday, June 1, 1821, at eleven o'clock, on the premises, THE Live and Dead FARMING STOCK, Part of

The Crowley brewery prospered and was acquired by the Burrell family on 24 March 1877. The following year Harry Percy Burrell married one of the daughters of A.C. Crowley. The brewery tower was built in 1901 when William Garton became a partner in the firm. The company merged with Watney Combe Reid & Co. in 1947.

Ashdell Bridge, with typically solid Victorian engineering, was built when the railway, which had reached Alton from Farnham in 1852, was extended to Winchester. The new line opened on 2 October 1865. The railway embankment to the left covers the site of Orps Mill.

The history of the low building on Normandy Street with the sun reflecting on the window can be traced back to the late 1600s. In 1736 it was leased by John Figg, knacker, and consisted of a house, stable, workshop and garden. Later occupants included a roper, a horse-collar maker, a staymaker, a carpenter and a sewing machine agent.

Christopher Ransom, seen here, came to Alton in 1924 and five years later bought Enticknap's cycle shop at 36 Normandy Street, seen here. With cycling being popular, and sited near the cinema, he also stored film-goers bikes and did repairs in the shed at the bottom of the garden. After he died his son, Bob, enlarged the shed into a shop.

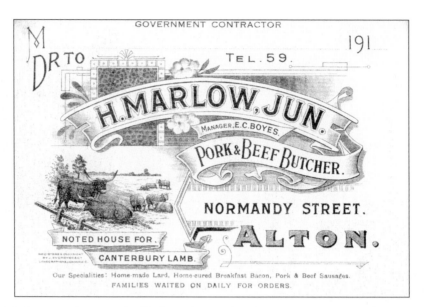

Henry Marlow was the son of Alfred Marlow, a thatcher. Henry's main trade seems to have been as a hay dealer – which is probably why the butchering business had a manager. In 1907, the 'well-ventilated butcher's shop, 17' x 14' with counter and window boards' and 'large cool slaughterhouse' were offered for sale.

The conversion in 1920 of Mr J. Martin's blacksmiths shop in Nether Street resulted in the Gospel Hall. After laying empty for some years, an office building named Normandy House was erected on the site which is behind the hairdressers shop on the corner of Nether Street and Normandy Street.

Further along Orchard Lane, eastwards from the Rising Sun, stood these five houses built in rat-trap bond – an 'economical' method of bricklaying common in the Alton area in the late nineteenth century. The bricks were laid on their edges rather than on their faces, so less were needed for the same amount of wall.

The landlord of the Rising Sun, Nether Street, was Harry Colston. He is seen here with his second wife, Harriet, on the occasion of the christening of their eldest son, Harry John, at St Lawrence Church on 15 June 1902. The driver of the Locomobile, made by Stanley Bros of the United States, was Jack Mathews, godfather to the infant.

The Alton Picture Theatre in Normandy Street opened in 1914 and was originally owned by the Phillips family of Aldershot. Silent movies were augmented by organ, piano or orchestra and were last screened on Saturday 7 March 1931. The building was quickly renovated and two days later it re-opened and 'talkies' hit Alton. The first film was *The Desert Song*.

There was an Independent chapel here in 1696, although a nonconformist group had been formed thirty-four years earlier. The present church opened for public worship on 14 April 1835 and the cottages that stood in front of it were removed ten years later. The church was extended in 1868 and celebrated its 250th anniversary on 23 October 1912.

Lock's Alley, previously known as Cole's Alley, ran between 41 Normandy Street and the chapel. Nimrod Lock pulled down an old barn at the end of the alley and built the forge in which he is pictured with his wife, Ninnie. There were four timber-framed cottages in the alley and they were painted by artist Fred Ireland in 1936.

In 1877 Thomas Knight, second from the left, was apprenticed to Charles Biddle and Edward Evans at their steam printing works in Normandy Street. A witness to this was Charles Moody, third from the left. Edward Evans is on the extreme right of the machine, a Bremner Wharfdale press.

The Normandy Street printing works was later run by Charles Moody, Edwin Moody and latterly by Harold Moody, although it was at 62 Normandy Street, not 61 which does not exist! The site next to the cinema gradually fell into disrepair during the illness of Harold Moody and was finally demolished early in 2002.

The system of tuition of masses of children by other partially educated children owes its origin to the British and Foreign School Society founded in 1810. The Alton British School began on 20 November 1843 and moved into the purpose-built Normandy Street premises in 1867, at that time on the edge of the town.

Later, the British School became Alton County Boys School and Alton Council Infants School, while the girls and infants remained at the National School, which became known as St Lawrence Church of England Girls' and Infants' School. Junior schools were set up after the 1918 Education Act which raised the school leaving age to fourteen.

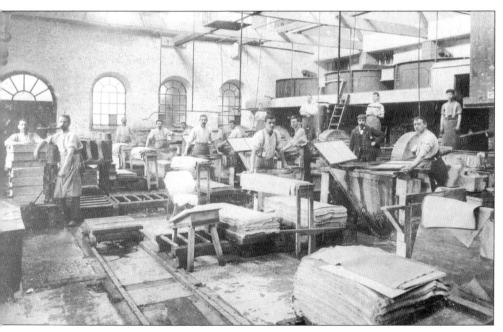

Spicer's Paper Mill was in Paper Mill Lane. The local paper of 27 March 1909 carried the sad news that 'Most of the men at the Paper Mill received notice on Saturday last that their engagement at Alton would terminate in a fortnight. Most of the men have not yet been informed whether they will be employed at the new mill in Kent'.

The children are sitting on the fountain near the junction of Anstey Road and Papermill Lane. It formerly stood in Crown Close but was moved to allow the building of the Cairn in 1920, and again later to the park. As well as helping his wife run the newsagent shop, William Halliday was a paper maker at the paper mill. His son, Charles, became a professor of music.

Edwin Loe had a business as a wine and spirit merchant at 60 High Street, while living next door at 58. He married Mary Jane Little, grand-daughter of Francis Little, a baker, grocer and corn and hop factor of Market Street. C.W. Hawkins was born in 16 Anstey Road, the house behind the horse, on 4 September 1907.

Mayfield Preparatory School was founded by Mary Shillinglow in November 1944 with ten children in a private house opposite the old General Hospital in Anstey Road. Later the school moved to The White House, 103 Anstey Road, opposite Anstey Park. The Brownie pack was formed on 19 May 1949.

The Mayfield cub pack was formed in 1955 and had their colours presented the following year. In time there were thirty-two cubs in four sixes – Nelson, Raleigh, Drake and Columbus. In 1994, on the fiftieth anniversary of the school, there were sixty-one boys and forty-seven girls on the roll. However, the school closed on 7 April 2000.

Plans for a new shop front to replace the bay window to the right of the door were approved in March 1936 and this marked the end of the tea rooms in Baverstock House, 106 High Street. D.J. Kemp & Sons did the building work for Mr J. Knight of Lenten Street, who opened a sweet shop that traded here for twenty-six years.

Built on part of the site of the former sawmill operated by the Pearce family, Urquhart & Son Ltd opened for business on 15 September 1955. The site has changed hands several times, but it has retained its connections with the motor trade although it no longer sells petrol. The signpost indicates that a main route to Basingstoke was along Ackender Road.

Ackender House on Butts Road was built of Selborne Stone in the 'rustic' style and the first owner seems to have been Dr Charles Stewart. He took the name for his house and school from a local piece of ancient woodland known as Ackner or Acknor. In 1861 the school had an assistant master and nineteen boys. The road alongside took its name from the house.

The auction sale of part of the Whitedown Estate, owned by George Woodruffe Gunner of Willhall Farm, took place on 26 October 1897. In all, some seventy plots of building land were offered, mainly along Queens Road with some on Basingstoke Road and a few on the end of Whitedown Road, later re-named Kings Road.

The wooden buildings of the original Princess Louise Hospital were brought into use by the Army in July 1903, before being taken over as the Lord Mayor Treloar Cripples Home and College five years later. The foundation stone for the first of the five blocks of replacement buildings, seen here, was laid on 22 October 1929.

The message on this postcard reads 'This is the Nurses Home <u>not</u> the Hospital. Second room from this end of basement is mine'. Known as Alexandra House, after Queen Alexandra, it was opened on 17 June 1914 by Queen Amélie of Portugal. Treloar's ran its own programme of training and issued its own certificate until 1936.

These five cottages in Wellhouse Lane, Beech, were owned by William Curtis of Alton in the mid-1800s. At that time they were at the end of the lane. In 1875, each cottage was insured for £60. When William died they were sold and John Gathorne Wood of Thedden Grange bought them.

In the 1840s these cottages were inhabited by families with local names – Adams, Forder, Munday, and Figg. James Figg was an Army pensioner who was paid an Army pension of 10s 6d a week. One cottage shown here was lived in by James Eade, a sawyer from Sussex, and his family for many years at the end of Victoria's reign.

In 1835 Sir Lawrence William Halsted CB of Thedden obtained, from Magdalen College Oxford, a licence to assign the lease of Beech Place Farm to John Wood of Horton House, Bradford, Yorkshire. At the end of the 1800s, W. Carter of Parkstone, Dorset, bought the farm and divided much of the land into building plots.

The caption on the back of this picture reads 'Old Farm Beech'. It shows cooking arrangements that would have been familiar to Raynold Goodyere of Beech who wrote his will in 1619. In 1695, Lewis Goodyer confirmed the lease he had made to William Barcome of a plot of ground at Wellhouse on which William had built a tenement.

The Order of Saint Paul is an Anglican Community living under the Benedictine Rule. The first building they built at the top of Kings Hill, Beech, was made of wattle. Later bricks were made from clay found in the grounds and these were used together with local flints. Here, in 1905, the memorial stone is being laid for the Abbey Church.

The service for the Dedication of the Abbey church of Our Lady and St John by the Bishop of Southampton took place on 4 September 1930. The Band of the Nautical School T S Mercury played during the day and, later, the Admiral of the Fleet, Sir Roger Keyes, opened the new Seaman's Pensionery for 'Helpless Merchant Seamen'.

Seamen's Friendly Society of
—— St. Paul. ——

THE ABBEY
ALTON,
HANTS.

Souvenir of Opening.

September 4th, 1930.

The architect of the new Abbey building was Sir Charles Nicholson and the general contractors were Messrs Kemp & Sons of Alton. Like most buildings in this area, the Abbey gained its water supply from the rain water that ran off the roofs into large tanks. An electric plant was also installed for lighting and for pumping the water.

In 1808, Thedden Manor Farm was offered for sale. It was bought by L.W. Halsted, who renamed it 'Phoenix Lodge' after his ship. In 1823 the house was described as 'a most desirable pleasant Family Residence' with suites of elegant apartments on the ground floor and suitable and well-arranged bed chambers on the first floor.

Two
Bentworth and Wield

In 1869, it was reported in the *Hampshire Herald* that St Mary's church, Bentworth, had been repaired and renewed in 1831 when £500 had been raised on the credit of the church rates. Over the next forty years £1,200 was spent on several items, including the addition of a new south aisle.

Now called Mulberry House, this was built as Bentworth Rectory. In a directory of 1878, it was described as a handsome residence built in 1818 and having beautiful grounds. The Revd Henry Staverton Mathews was both patron and incumbent at that time.

The entrance to Hall Farm was said, by Nikolas Pevsner and David Lloyd in their *Buildings of Hampshire and the Isle of Wight*, to date from the early 1300s. The mouldings of the archway are especially characteristic of this time. The house was probably started by William de Aule who had been Constable of Farnham Castle.

Also known as Old Manor Farm, work on the main building may have been continued by William du Aule's widow, Matilda, as she was granted the right to have a private chapel around 1333. This is thought to be the building on the right of the picture. A solar wing and staircase were added to the house later.

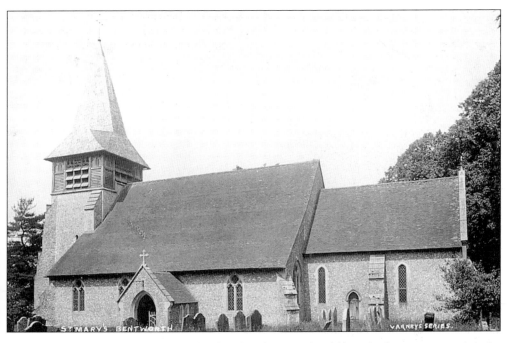

In 1887 it was resolved that, if possible, the church tower should be rebuilt as a memorial to the late rector – the Revd H.S. Mathews. If a sufficient sum for this purpose could not be raised a fence was to be placed round the base of the tower and a less costly memorial erected.

The farm buildings on the right are part of Hall Farm. In the distance can be seen The Star public house. The house on the left of the pond belonged to James Ward, a plumber, painter and glazier. James died in 1864, but the Ward family remained in the village for over 130 years with James junior continuing the plumbing business and Arthur being a land surveyor.

Bentworth School was built in 1848, at a cost of £600, on part of the glebe. It consisted of one schoolroom and a house for the teacher. In 1871, the school was enlarged by the addition of a second classroom for infants and a gallery. The schoolmaster in the late 1800s was Charles Penson who taught here for thirty-eight years, retiring in 1918.

The two oldest bells both date from 1601 and were, along with one dated 1607, cast by Joseph Carter of Whitechapel. The newest bell shown here was made in 1615 by Henry Knight of Reading. A fifth bell was added in memory of Dr William George Cazalet, rector for almost forty years and a sixth bell was acquired in 1988.

On Saturday 6 March 1926, Bentworth Football Team played Holybourne at Bentworth. Holybourne scored first but Bentworth proved too strong and were soon level. In the second half Bentworth, well supported by their defence, scored three more goals. Exactly a month before, Bentworth had played Bentley and won 3-0.

In 'The Great Blizzard' of December 1927 – the snowdrifts were so high that telegraph poles were nearly buried – the porcelain insulators were within touching distance. Mr W. Berry, the Alton postmaster, told the local paper that it was the worst time he had experienced during his forty years in the post office.

This picture of Ham Corner appeared in the *Hampshire Herald and Alton Gazette* on 6 January 1928. The caption commented on the half buried signpost pointing to Wield. There was hardly a village in the area that was not isolated from wheeled traffic for at least a week. More misery followed when the thaw set in, with flooding in many places.

Bentworth Lodge is situated near the Alton to Basingstoke Road. It was hardly a lodge though – with seven members of the family, nine indoor servants and a Swiss governess in residence on census night in 1891! Originally called Binstead Hill, it was bought by Captain Frederick Stephens JP, who had retired from the 2nd Life Guards.

Gaston Grange was built in the 1870s by Colonel Gordon Maynard Gordon-Ives on the site of Gaston Cottage. It remained in the family until 1922, when the *Hampshire Herald and Alton Gazette* announced the sale of furniture, because of the sale of the mansion. Bentworth Hall was also owned by the Gordon-Ives family.

Burkham Farm belonged to the Coulthard family and contained 478 acres. The stock listed in this sale document gives an idea of the mixed farming undertaken by Stephen Dicker. He died in Bentworth less than two months after this sale and was buried in South Warnborough, where he had been born nearly seventy-five years before.

Although known as Bentworth and Lasham Station, the building actually lay in Lasham parish. It was one mile from Bentworth village, on the Alton to Basingstoke line. In 1932, the Alton Rural District Council received a letter from the Southern Railway Traffic Managers notifying them that it had been decided to close the railway line for passenger traffic.

After a visit to Wield church in 1905, the Diocesan Architect, Mr Cancellor, reported that the cracks in both the north and south walls were of a very serious nature and that, unless they were attended to promptly, the walls could collapse. It was decided that the church bell would not be rung as the vibration would affect the cracks!

The church of St James contains a large effigy of William Wallop, son of Oliver Wallop. William was mayor of Southampton three times and High Sheriff of Hampshire. His third wife, Margery, erected the alabaster monument after her husband died in 1617. Her effigy also lies under a canopy on which stand two cherubs.

The cottage on the right, which is shown on the Tithe Map of 1839, was owned by James Windebank, a wheelwright. He, his brother, William, and mother, Elizabeth, lived in one part of the building and George Day, an agricultural labourer, lived in the other part with his wife, Amelia.

The white building in the middle of the picture was Wield Primitive Methodist chapel. It was built in 1848 and seated eighty-six people with standing room for forty-four more. In 1851 John Cox, a labourer from Wiltshire, was the chapel steward.

Three

Lasham and Shalden

In 1859 St Mary's church in Lasham was described as 'a plain structure, which was rebuilt in 1679 and repaired in 1840'. It was small but did not need to be any bigger, as the rector answered to an inquiry from the bishop in 1725, 'we have about three births, two burials, and sometimes never a marriage in three or four years'.

The buildings on the left belong to Church Farm. In 1881, Mary Parker, the widow of James Parker, lived here. Her brother-in-law, John Parker, was nearby at Manor Farm. There were three other farms in Lasham – Hill Farm, Parsonage Farm and New Farm.

The house and blacksmith's shop, on the right, belonged to William Harrison in 1838. In the same year, the large house on the left was the Parsonage House. In 1924, tenders were received for a new rectory and this building became known as Lasham House.

This cottage is the old post office. In 1903, the Lasham post office was run by Mrs Elizabeth Vickers, widow of Edward Vickers. Postal orders could be issued here, but not paid and the nearest telegraph office was Bentworth, two miles away. By 1907 Mrs Wright had taken over.

At a Vestry Meeting held in Shalden on 31 March 1864, it was resolved that 'taking into consideration the want of accommodation provided by the parish church, and that it is in much need of repair; it is desirable to pull it down, and rebuild it according to the plans provided by Mr Colson and approved by the bishop.'

It was agreed that the site for the new church would be the unused portion of the churchyard, between the old church and the north-western boundary. It was noted in 1865 that the contract with the builders was signed by Mr John Wood of Thedden Grange, Lord of the Manor of Shalden, and owner of almost the whole parish.

In 1912, the cottage nearest the road had a living room, pantry, two bedrooms and a woodshed and the rent was 2s a week, which included the rates. The right-hand cottage, with one room upstairs and one room downstairs, was let to George Oliver for 1s 6d a week. The building on the left is Gregory's Farm which was owned by Mr Wood.

When Mr C. Allen, the new headteacher, took charge of Shalden School in June 1891, he found that 'the work of the children in Standard I is very poor, cannot form their letters, very little knowledge of arithmetic or tables'. In September, he noted that children were absent as their parents required their assistance in the harvest fields.

On 6 November 1908, E. Godfrey, the Diocesan Inspector, reported that excellent work was being done in the little school. The children's interest had been aroused and stimulated. Their manner was quiet and reverant, and their knowledge of the subjects taught was very satisfactory.

In October 1936, Sergeant Tom Cass was appointed to take charge of Alton Police Station. He is seen here (on the left) early in his career as a constable with his father, a police inspector on the Isle of Wight, and his brother Edwin, also a police constable.

Tom Cass moved to Shalden in 1939. An Honorary Life Member and Vice-President of the Old English Sheep Dog Club, he is pictured here with 'Shep' (Shepherd's Choice). The publication in May 1987 of *Tom Cass - Mayor of Shalden* by the late Anne Pitcher, gave the fascinating story of the life and times of this well known and highly respected man.

56

Four

Holybourne

In the religious census of 1851, Mr Merriman, a temporary curate, replied that 'the 30 March was the Sacrament Sunday and on such days the Congregation is always less than on other occasions. As I am only a temporary I have no means of making a more full return than this'. The morning attendance had only been 182 instead of the more usual 310.

A plaque inside the church records that the spire was erected to the memory of Thomas and Elizabeth Howard who were the most devoted and self-sacrificing parents of Edith Emma Judge. They had been married in Holybourne church in 1836 and Elizabeth, who was the daughter of John and Elizabeth Bradley, had been baptised there twenty-two years earlier.

The clock in the tower was erected by public subscription to commemorate the Coronation of His Majesty King George V on 22 June 1911. Stephen Randall was the honorary secretary of the Coronation Committee, Revd B.W. Peacock, the vicar, J.F. Complin and Major R.E. Pole, the churchwardens. The bells were restored in 1951.

In 1873, an insurance policy was taken out on the private brick dwelling house known as The Priory, which was in the tenure of Joseph James. It was valued at £500 and the stable and coachhouse nearby were valued at £100. By 1891, The Priory was the home of Edward Hall, the second son of Henry Hall, the Alton brewer.

The Lawn was bought by Mrs Gaskell, an author, with money earned from her writing. She died here on Sunday 12 November 1865 and the house was still owned by the Gaskell family in the early 1900s. The occupier of the house in 1895 was Captain Hon. Archibald Robert Hewitt RN retired.

Owned by the nearby Complin's Brewery of Holybourne until it was taken over by Farnham United, the Prince of Wales contained a bar, tap-room and smoking room as well as a detached clubroom. It was formerly called the Compasses and the landlords included Benjamin Arnold, Elizabeth Clark and Henry Collop.

Stephen Randall was a grocer and draper as well as selling boots and crockery. His adverts boasted 'Malt & Hops, Corn, Meal & Pollard. Ready-made Clothing. Boots & Shoes. Families waited on Daily with Bread. Carts deliver daily in Alton'. Joseph Tompsett, who had run a similar business in Bentley, was the previous shopkeeper.

The cottages on the left were inhabited in 1881 by labourers – several of them over sixty-five years of age, but still not yet retired. The house with the gables and sign was Elizabeth Smith's. She and her sister were bakers. Next to the White Hart lived Jesse Spiers, a labourer at one of the nearby water mills, with his wife and seven children.

As can be seen from this picture, the White Hart public house sold Crowley's Alton Ales. The Alton brewery already owned it in 1842 when the landlord was Benjamin Burningham, a carpenter. When he died in 1849, his widow Sarah took over. By 1859 their son John, who was also a carpenter, had the license although his mother lived for another six years.

J. Wiltshire took a quarterly tenancy for the White Hart Hotel in September 1900. He paid a rent of £50 a year to the owners – Crowley & Co. The premises contained a private bar, club room, public bar, sitting room, hall, commercial room and seven bedrooms. The outbuildings included an acetylene house, stables, a loose box and a coach house.

The staff at Complins brewery were pictured by George Frost, a photographer from Alton. The workers at the brewery included James White, Joe White, James Martin, Fred Arnold, Harry Cook and Alfred Goddard. Thomas Tigg was a drayman and Charles Watts an engine driver.

The Complin family, probably in 1869. At that time, the children of Walter John and his wife, Fanny, would have been John Fowler aged ten, Fanny aged eight and Walter aged three. The family property was called 'Fishers' and Walter J. Complin was a brewer, master malster, farmer and hop grower.

In 1891, 'The Attractive Residential and Business Property Known as "Neatham Mill", comprising large and superior residence, charming Garden, Pleasure Grounds and Paddock; capital WATER CORN MILL, with wheel of extraordinary size and power, and unlimited water supply' was offered for sale. It was later bought by Henry Denyer of Thursley Mill, Godalming, Surrey.

Neatham Upper Mill Farm was acquired by Jesse Marlow, a hay and straw merchant in 1918. The property included the farmhouse, water mill, outbuildings, land, 'the whole of the bed or soil of the River Wey where the same runs through the said lands' and all the fishing rights. Sadly, the mill burnt down in the 1930s although the house still stands.

Alfred Stevens' cottage on the right was owned by the Misses C. and E. James of The Shrubbery in 1911. The ladies were the daughters of John James, formerly of the Admiralty. The next house and butcher's shop belonged to Ada Warner. After her husband, James Whiten Warner died in 1908 she continued to run the business.

Although the houses on the left look quite modern, in the early 1900s they still had pail closets and shared a communal wash house. The house nearer the centre of the picture was the post office in 1911 and the sub-postmaster was David Bone. He had been born at East Worldham and became a blacksmith.

Some of the problems of teaching in a Hampshire village school were highlighted by this report of the Annual Examination of Andrew's School in 1886 – 'I find that on account of the prevalence of measles in the early part of the spring, and latterly, the employment of the children in the hopgardens, your school has had to contend with a good deal of irregularity'.

By 1895, Robert Dymoke 'successor to W. Berry, agricultural implement maker, wheelwright and smith' lived and worked here. The premises contained a sawpit shed, smithy, shoeing shed, carpenter's shop, eight elms and two chestnut trees as well as the house. In 1928, a picture of Holybourne Smithy appeared in *The Times* – it was used to illustrate an article on 'The Road'.

A directory of 1931 advertised – 'Holybourne Service Station (R.J. Chase, proprietor), motor engineer, petrol, oils and agent for Coventry Eagle motor cycles.' Later it was described as 'a tin shed with a petrol pump'! The premises were acquired by C.O.G. Smith who rebuilt them and the grand opening of the 'modern up-to-date garage and service station' took place on 2 July 1966.

Five
Froyle and Bentley

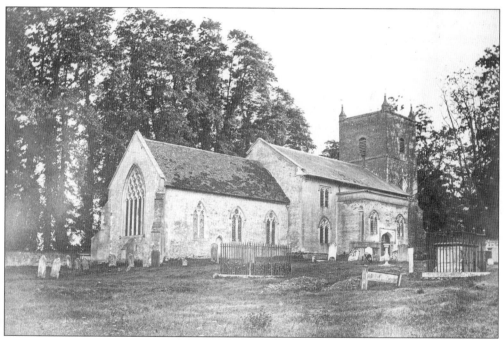

A general vestry of the parish of Froyle was held in 1811 to consider the dangerous and dilapidated state of St Mary's church. James Harding, a surveyor from Farnham, reported that the effectual repairs would cost almost as much as rebuilding. It was decided to replace the body of the church – but not the chancel or tower.

A sale catalogue of 1885 described Froyle Place as a spacious substantial family mansion. It was said to have been built of stone quarried on the estate with strong lead roofs and picturesque gables and to have been surrounded by well-arranged gardens and pleasure grounds. The catalogue continued – 'the air is fine and salubrious'.

The Froyle School log book began with an entry for 2 November 1868: 'The schools in this village were formally opened today. There was afternoon service in the church when the vicar of Alton was the preacher; after service the children and their parents assembled in the school rooms, when the schools were opened by the vicar of the parish'.

Upper Froyle post office, showing one of the small statues that have given Froyle its name of 'The Village of the Saints'. This one is of St Hubert. Sir Hubert Miller, the lord of the manor, brought them back from Italy. In 1927, Mrs Clara Knight was the post mistress for Upper Froyle.

Known locally as the 'Roman stile', this carved stone slab lay on the north side of the Alton – Farnham road, opposite Shrubbery House. When the road was altered in the 1960s, it was re-positioned at the side of the layby nearby. Sadly, the stile has deteriorated a great deal since this picture was taken in the early 1900s.

Pond Cottages are in Husseys Lane in Lower Froyle, opposite the village pond. The three cottages nearest the camera were owned by Mrs Mary Watkins of The Highways at the time of the Froyle tithe map of 1847 and one of the occupiers was William Faulkener. On the right of the picture was a house and smithy.

In 1885, Froyle Mill was leased by William Young. The three-story building had two 16ft breast wheels which drove four pairs of French burr stones. The mill house contained drawing and dining rooms, an office, store room, kitchen, cellar, pantry and five bedrooms. In the garden was a greenhouse and a vinery.

Bentley church from the north. The chapel to the left is medieval as are the two light-coloured windows in the North Aisle, relocated to the new aisle in the restoration of 1890. Mr Lang, then the vicar, studied at Trinity College, Cambridge. He came to Bentley via Pembrokeshire and Suffolk, as well as nearby Farnham and Frensham in Surrey.

The existing Perrylands house is of nineteenth century origin, but the estate is much older and is first identifiable at the death in 1334 of John de Westcote. A series of prominent owners included Sir Richard Holt, Sir Edward Berkeley and William Blount, fourth Lord Mountjoy. In 1806 the stock-in-trade and utensils were insured for £1,000.

Bentley Street from Bentley Green which (with other common land) was enclosed by Act of Parliament in 1851. The two right-hand houses and the high wall are still there but the left-hand, light-coloured house has gone, as has the cedar tree from which Cedar Cottage was named. To the left of the low wall are Hole Lane and the Memorial Hall.

The local Home Guard unit in front of the Bentley Memorial Hall. On the wall is the war memorial, which lists twenty-four of their comrades who died in the First World War. Later, sixteen more names were added. The Hall was built in 1923 and enlarged in 1952.

The Tompsett family were shopkeepers in Bentley for over half a century, as drapers, grocers, coal merchants, wine and spirit merchants. For most of that time they were sub-postmasters too. In 1881, Israel Tompsett, the proprietor, employed six men and two boys; his father, Joseph, who had previously kept the Bentley shop, was a draper and grocer in nearby Holybourne.

Believed to date from the seventeenth century, the Bull may have become a public house when the adjacent turnpike road was constructed in the mid-eighteenth century. Courage's, the brewers, acquired the Bull when they took over Farnham United Breweries in 1927. In the early twentieth century, the Bull was kept by Mrs Mary Karn and then Mrs Fanny Karn.

The Railway Arms Hotel, Bentley Ha...

Despite the caption, The Railway Arms (like Bentley Station) is actually in Binsted parish. Now a residence called Bentley House, the former public house doubtless dates from the arrival of the railway from Farnham in 1852. One of several pubs locally held by members of the Karn family, The Railway Arms was kept before the First World War by Fanny Karn.

This fine two-aisled barn, is believed to belong to Marelands. The curved braces, between the tie-beams and the aisle posts, being concave upwards, suggest a seventeenth-century date. The collection of farm machinery includes a traditional four-wheeled wagon, a tip-cart, a mechanical hay rake, a dairy cart and a corn crusher stands in the doorway.

Six

Binsted

Until 1854, Binsted church, seen here from the south-west, was a chapel of Alton parish. It was restored and re-pewed in 1863/64. The vicar from 1895 was the Revd W.G.G. Gosling. After Marlborough College, he studied in America, and from 1880 to 1889 held a number of appointments in Tennessee before coming back to England.

Inside Binsted church is this fine monument to Richard de la Bere of Westcote. He wears full chain-mail, a surcoat, leather shin-guards, and has a sword and shield. His head lies on a cushion and his feet rest on a lion. In 1332 he established a Chantry with a priest to sing mass daily in a chapel which he had newly built onto the church.

The West Court estate was held of the Manor of Alton Westbrook at a rent of £2 10s and can be traced as far back as 1333 when Richard de la Bere (whose tomb is shown above) held it. The present house dates from the sixteenth century, though much altered, and is said to have some good Elizabethan panelling.

Church Cottage, on the left of this picture, stands opposite the parish church and has a 'jettied' or projecting upper story. Roxford Farm house, on the right, is probably of seventeenth-century origin. The Victorian letter box in the long wall between Church Cottage and Roxford Farm is still in use.

The Wickham Institute, on the left, was erected around 1901 and conveyed by Mrs Sophia Wickham to the Winchester Diocesan Trustees – the predecessors of the Winchester Diocesan Board of Finance – in that year. To the right of the Institute, and end-on to the road, is the former Kings Arms public house, now called Kings Bounty.

The Cedars was rebuilt around 1926 following a fire. Formerly a Farnham United Breweries' house, it was acquired by Courage in 1927. James Henry Clements was landlord here for thirty-six years.

Variously known as the Parsonage or the Rectory, the ordnance plan names this multi-period house as Parsonage Farm. The core shows signs of diaper work (diagonal patterns in darker bricks) on the gable-end. A Faculty for demolition was granted in 1885, parts of the building being 'in a very bad state'. A new house, 'Kings Chantry', was built on the site in 1910/11.

A fulling mill existed at Millcourt from at least the later sixteenth century. In 1699 Nicholas Gates of Alton and Nicholas Wheeler of Millcourt agreed to rebuild it in stone. By 1913 it had become derelict. Only some footings and a sluice remain of the mill, but the millhouse is still standing.

The present Isington Mill may be eighteenth century in date, but a mill was certainly there a century earlier, described in 1602 as 'two watermills' (i.e. two pairs of millstones) 'under one roof'. The mill was formerly the home of Field Marshal Montgomery, who converted it into a house. More recently Charles and Naomi Bowen restored the machinery to working order.

This unusual looking house was built as a semaphore tower, part of the never-completed line of Admiralty signal stations from London to Plymouth. Construction began in 1829, but was abandoned in 1831; whether the semaphore apparatus itself was ever installed is not known.

Alice Holt Lodge was built some time between 1800 and 1816, when the office of Keeper of the Forest was abolished. The house was then leased to private occupants until the Second World War when it was requisitioned. After the war it passed to the Forestry Commission, and now houses the department's research station.

Seven

Kingsley and Selborne

On Saturday 21 January 1905, the ancient church of St Nicholas was re-opened after its restoration. It must have been in need of this work as it was described, in the Victoria County History, as being 'little better than a brick barn'. The last Divine Service held here had been on Sunday 6 August 1876 and it was then used for funeral services.

The new parish church of All Saints was consecrated on 8 August 1876 by Dr Harold Brown, Bishop of Winchester. In the early English style, the church was built by Messrs Dyers of Alton using Selborne stone relieved by black Weaver's Down stone at the sole cost of Hon. John Thomas Dutton, the Lord of the Manor.

The interior walls of the new church were faced with Fareham bricks in two shades of red and Aldershot white bricks pointed with black mortar. The string courses and dressings were of Bath stone and the red and black paving tiles were made by Minton, Hollins & Co. The east window was erected as a memorial to his parents by Hon. John Dutton.

Revd Charles Bingham Walsh MA held the joint livings of Kingsley and Binsted from 1854 until his resignation in 1895, when he was in his late seventies. He was born in Dublin and his wife came from Banff in Scotland. Unlike his successor, Revd Walsh chose to live here in Kingsley. In the early 1900s, the parish was served by a succession of curates-in-charge.

Albert Downer came to teach at Kingsley School in June 1874, having been born on the Isle of Wight twenty-two years previously. In 1881 his niece, Helen Fowler, was a pupil teacher at the school. Mr Downer stayed for nearly forty years, retiring in 1913. He was also the organist and choirmaster at the church.

The Allden family farmed Malthouse Farm for nearly thirty years. They took an active part in the life of the parish, being sidesmen and church wardens. At the time this picture was taken, William Allden occupied the 414 acres of Malthouse, Osborne's and Gander's Farms – all owned by Mr Dutton.

The train seen here ran on the Bordon Light Railway which went from Bentley to Bordon. This branch line was built to serve the military camps in the area and opened in 1905. The only other stop was Kingsley Halt and the line closed on 4 April 1966.

Selborne Old Vicarage was built in 1845 by the then vicar, Revd F.J. Parsons, over the surviving Tudor cellars of a previous house. An earlier vicar, John Farroll, having been ejected from the living, retired to Guildford but later spent six months in the Marshalsea Prison in 1669 for his refusal to take the Corporation Oath.

The three single lancet windows in Selborne church are nineteenth century, but the triple-lancet of the south chapel, on the left, is ancient. Gilbert White, the eighteenth-century naturalist, lies in the churchyard. The lane in the foreground leads down the valley towards Priory Farm, the site of Selborne Priory suppressed in 1484.

The Short Lythe and the Long Lythe cloak the steep northern side of the valley of the Oakhanger Stream, on its way from the village to Selborne Priory and Oakhanger. On the southern side of the valley is the wood called Great Dorton. Here in the Lythes Gilbert White and his brother, Thomas, studied crickets.

The square known as the Plestor was granted to Selborne Priory in 1271 by Adam Gurdon. Perhaps the heart of Selborne village, the church is away to the right. It was here that a mob of some 200 'Swing' rioters gathered on 22 November 1830 before first attacking the poorhouse and then threatening the vicarage.

The Maxwell family had this shop, at the side of the Plestor, from 1832 until 1948, and traded in grocery and general stores. In 1888 they were advertising Gorgonzola ceese, of which they had imported 'a prime lot', at 8½d per lb, or by the whole 7lb cheese at 8d per lb.

The garden front of The Wakes before the addition of the storey over the great hall and library in the 1890s. The original house is probably early sixteenth century, but is surrounded by many later extensions. Gilbert White lived here from 1729 or 1730, until his death in 1793. In 1844 the house was acquired by Professor Thomas Bell, a zoologist, who died in 1880.

The garden front, sometime after 1902. An appeal was launched in 1954 to acquire the house as a memorial to Gilbert White. With help from a fund set up by the Oates family, The Wakes was opened by the Duke of Wellington in September 1955 to the honour of Gilbert White and of Francis and Captain Lawrence Oates, travellers, naturalists and explorers.

The Queen's Hotel was formerly called the Queen's Arms and before that the Compasses. In 1800 the property belonged to John Hawkins of the Alton Brewery. Courage & Co. took over the Alton Brewery and its tied houses in 1903.

The shop and post office on the right is now Selborne Antiques. The Selborne Arms is beyond, also on the right and between them is Bush House.

Selborne Street looking north-east towards the Plestor. The 'vertical crazy paving' style of wall-facing on the house left of centre, was popular in the nineteenth century. The Queen's Hotel is in the middle-distance on the right.

Besides running the post office, Mr John Legg functioned as draper and grocer, baker, corn and provision merchant, stationer, ironmonger, tobacconist, boot warehouse and general stores.

Alongside the Selborne Arms are the cottages that later became the Bush Tea Room – sadly now closed. It would be very difficult nowadays to find Selborne Street so empty of traffic!

90

The roadside Lion fountain at the south end of the village was presented in 1891. The door on the right conceals a hydraulic ram (an ingenious form of water pump which requires no power source beyond the water-flow) which fed a village water supply to four taps along the main street.

Selborne. The Zigzags

The 'Zigzag' path was constructed by Gilbert White and his brother, John. The path rises some 200 feet up the face of Selborne Hanger, to Selborne Common on top of the hill, and greatly eases the gradient of the hillside.

On the edge of Selborne Common, at the top of the 'Zigzag' and overlooking the valley, is the Obelisk or Wishing Stone, placed there by Gilbert White as a landscape feature. The stone is a large piece of Sarsen, silica-cemented 'puddingstone', found at several places locally.

Perhaps one of the last plough-teams of oxen in the area, this photograph was taken at Norton Farm which lies on the road from Selborne to Alton. This road was created in the middle of the nineteenth century, as the earlier route was indirect and treacherous in bad weather.

Eight

East and West Worldham and Hartley Mauditt

In the 1860s, the nave and chancel of East Worldham church were restored and it had, among other things – a new roof, east window, paving tiles and marble columns. The total cost of more than £1,400 included £70 to the architect, David Brandon, and £1,222 to Messrs Dyers of Alton, the builders. The first service, after all the work was complete, took place on 29 July 1866.

Now a private house, these hop kilns were part of Old House Farm, which belonged to Winchester College. This property was leased from them by the Heighes family for 120 years from 1612 and then by the Christmas family for the next 120 years. In 1851, William Christmas employed thirteen labourers to help him farm his 290 acres.

Partly hidden by the trees is the Three Horse Shoes public house. It was licensed in 1834 and substantially rebuilt, in brick and stone, in 1884. In a sale document of 1930, it was described as 'well-frequented' and was let to Courages at £100 a year. The house adjoining was called 'Huntons' and its garden now forms the car park to the front of the pub.

or much of Queen Victoria's reign, the publican of the Three Horse Shoes was Henry
Newman. A local man, he described himself as a blacksmith, shopkeeper and victualler! He
ied in 1890, aged ninety-four. By the time of this picture the blacksmith's shop, seen here, was
et to Thomas Wood and later to Walter Jack Wood.

Henry Newman's son, another Henry, leased the Three Horse Shoes to John Fowler Complin
1908 for seven years. A year later, Complin leased his brewery including these premises to
arnham United Breweries. Henry junior died in 1922, aged eighty-eight.

At the top of Worldham Hill the white gateposts on the left mark the drive into the vicarage. At the end of the 1800s, the vicar was Revd George Hunter Fell who had been born in Henley-on-Thames. The building on the far left is still extant.

East Worldham Church School was built in 1864. When Adeline Farshaw arrived in Januar 1890 to be the school mistress, she found that order and discipline were bad. Of the sixty-eigh children on the roll, only forty-seven were present during her first week. In February sh reported that it was impossible to follow the regular course of lessons as there was no chalk an not enough slates.

The large building on the right of Worldham Hill was the Wesleyan chapel. It was granted a certificate for religious worship on 27 May 1878. In 1891, George Othen was a local preacher as well as being a bricklayer. The chapel stopped being used for worship in 1937 and has since been demolished.

West Worldham church was described as a small plain structure. Gradually it fell into disrepair and by 1878 was said to be ruinous and not used for services. A year later, William Turvill wrote to the Bursar of Winchester College complaining that the position regarding the church was a disgrace, it having been closed for over five years.

In the west window of St Nichola's church is some old coloured glass including a mermaid – part of the arms of Nicholas Mason, a royalist, who lived in the village during the Commonwealth. Also in the church are several tablets to the Hammond family who farmed locally in the 1700s and 1800s.

In 1972, permission was sought to strip and re-tile part of the roof, repair the wall, render and repair or renew the stonework to several windows as well as the bellcote. Work on the chancel and roof had already been completed the year before.

Every Michaelmas Day (29 September), £1 was paid to the minister of Hartley Mauditt for preaching on death, resurrection or judgement and 30s given to the poor people who had come to listen. Forty years later, the rector announced that the church and churchyard were being repaired and that all things necessary were to be provided in a sumptuous manner.

In 1725, it was reported that the number of souls in the parish was about sixty. This included sixteen men and their wives, three widowers and widows, twenty-seven young people (grown up and servants) and fourteen children. There would be about one marriage, one burial and two baptisms a year. By 1801, the population had dropped to fifty-seven but rose to eighty-seven in 1851.

Known as the Round House, this building was a lodge to Hartley Mauditt House and was built long before the direct Alton to Selborne road was opened. In 1881 William Cooper, a shepherd, lived here with his family. At that time, over one third of the twenty-two households in the village had the surname of Cooper.

Gilbert White, who lived at Selborne, described the old sunken lane from there to Alton, via Hartley Mauditt, as being reduced sixteen to eighteen feet below the level of the fields in many places and looking more like a watercourse than a road. He added that 'these gloomy scenes affright the ladies when they peep down into them from the paths above'.

Nine

Newton Valence, East Tisted and Farringdon

Stephen Warner, in his book on Newton Valence, quoted the following verse:
'One thousand Eight Hundred and Seventy-one, This happy work in our Tower begun;
In days gone by we can all agree, That Newton bells rang "One! Two! Three!"
Two more bells were later added, making five.'

Despite the assertion of the caption, Pelham Place lies in the parish of Newton Valence. In 1782 an agreement was drawn up with William Dawes of Alton, carpenter, for the building of the mansion for Captain (later Admiral) Thomas Dumar esq. Twenty-one years later, the old front of the house was taken down and a Gothic one erected.

The nearest of the cottages shown here was known as Pond House in 1840. It and the smaller cottage next to it were owned by Henry Chawner who lived at the Manor House. He was said to have been an official of the Mint in London who married a banker's heiress. The Pond looks quite small here, but it covered almost an acre at the time of the tithe map of 1840.

The religious census of 1851 recorded that the church of St James, East Tisted, had been recently rebuilt by J.W. Scott and consecrated in 1848. The average size of the congregation was said to be about 130 and every parishioner had a sitting. This was only ten more than in 1725.

The cottages lying alongside the Gosport Road were inhabited by outdoor workers on the Rotherfield Estate including gardeners, a carpenter and a stone mason. The black and white houses in the centre were almshouses which had been erected by Thomas and Septimus Scott in 1879.

This large Victorian house was East Tisted Rectory and was home to Revd Frederick Howlett from 1869 to 1896. He died in 1908, having moved to Bristol. By 1901, Revd Arthur Hutchings had taken over. It is now known as Tisbury House.

The present Rotherfield Park was built for James Scott between 1815 and 1821, by J.T. Parkinson and was then altered in the 1860s and again in 1893. In 1955 Norris Thrower recalled seeing, when he first came to Alton from London, a pair of zebras harnessed tandem and drawing a small dogcart from Rotherfield Park into Alton!

The Meon Valley railway line opened on 1 June 1903. East Tisted was the first station after Alton on the journey south to Fareham and the sign states 'East Tisted for Selborne'. The last public train passed through here on the evening of 5 February 1955 and the station became a private house.

In 1765 the rector of Farringdon, William Roman, reported that he resided at his other parsonage of Clatford but that the curate of Farringdon lived in Selborne, the next parish. That curate was, of course, Gilbert White who served this church from 1760 to 1785. The rector in the early 1800s was the Revd John Benn whose sister was a friend of Jane Austen.

The porch on the right belongs to Old School House. Morning school was from nine until twelve and afternoon school was between two and five in the summer, and between one-thirty and four in the winter. The holidays consisted of eight weeks at harvest, one week at Christmas, Easter Monday and Tuesday, Whit Monday and Tuesday and every Saturday.

According to Pevsner, Massey's Folly eclipses the church and the whole village. He described it as being built of fiery red brick and terracotta. In 1955 Farringdon Parish Council wanted to buy the building, but they needed the consent of the county council in order to take a loan of £1,000. The cost was £450 plus £500 for roof repairs, leaving £50 to install modern drainage.

In the 1920s, the Old Barn, as it was then known, was the home of Miss Madelaine Sharp, a dog breeder. By 1935, Miss Emma Hobson was running the refreshment rooms called the Old Barn Café. Four years later, Miss Florence Mabel and Miss Mary Alexandrina Forester had taken over the business.

Now known as Jordans, this was originally two cottages. One of them was used by the Farringdon Working Mens' Club and Reading Room. At the annual meeting in 1891, it was stated that the accounts were very satisfactory – showing a balance, after all expenses, of 4s 1d. On 10 February they held their annual supper and partook of a 'sumptuous spread'.

This picture must be from around 1935 as the proprietors of the grocers and post office were G. and K. Curtis. An earlier owner, Mr Phelps, had his cellar flooded to a depth of four to five feet when the snow thawed after the blizzard of 1927. A surveyor investigated and reported that nothing could be done as the water was spring water rising from the nearby gravel pit.

The Royal Oak was a Courage house run by Frank Simmons. The Royal Oak Garage opened in the 1930s and its proprietor was Tom Winters. His annual petrol licence was for 1,500 gallons and 1 cwt of carbide, and his telephone number was Tisted 39. The post office had the number Farringdon 1 in 1931, but by 1935 it also had a Tisted number – Tisted 35.

Ten
Chawton

In March 1871, according to a letter written by A.W. Blomfield, architect, 'a boy passing the church heard a crackling, and not seeing anything through the keyhole he looked through a side window when he saw flames in the gallery on the north side and gave the alarm'. The church had just had new heating apparatus installed and was to have been re-opened later that day!

The Right Revd Samuel Wilberforce, Bishop of Winchester, opened the renovated church on 20 July 1872, even though the tower had not been finished. It had been necessary to rebuild the body of the church and the cost was said to be about £2,300. After the service, the married poor of the parish 'sat down to an excellent dinner'.

Edward Knight insured his mansion 'Chawton House' for £10,000 in 1873. Eight years later, Montague Knight, aged thirty-six, his wife, brother, brother-in-law and four nieces and nephews were here on census night. They were attended by a butler, footman, two grooms, a housekeeper, cook, two house maids, kitchen maid, scullery maid and two nursery maids!

These four cottages, known as The Malt Houses, only had four rooms each. In 1891, one of them contained nine people – Francis Triggs, a sawyer, his wife and seven children – six boys and one girl. Occupants of the other cottages included Elizabeth Andrews, a widow, whose husband, Richard, had been a gardener, James Stacey, a carter, and William Adams, a storeman.

In the late 1800s, the headmaster was James Pritchard who had been born in Wheaton Aston in Staffordshire. When the school inspectors visited they reported that the discipline was very good and the writing very fair – though scarcely neat enough. The infants could read and write well, but had lost ground in their summing. Order and needlework were good, but the singing was only fair.

The closest dwellings are known as Pond Cottages and contain a pair of well-preserved crucks. In the late 1800s, William Oakley, an agricultural labourer, lived in the furthest of the row together with his wife, three sons and three daughters. One son had become mechanised and was a steam ploughman.

Although this road junction looks very peaceful here, it was the meeting point of the A31 road from Winchester and Southampton and the A32 from Portsmouth. Regular traffic jams would build up, especially on a Sunday evening in the summer, when people would be making their way back to the London area after a day out.

The living van on the left was made by Wright & Son who had a yard at The Butts, Alton. The van was used by a team of roadmen whose steam roller would tow it and a water bowser to wherever they were working around the district. Here they were filling in Chawton village pond.

Probably built in the 1700s, this house was used by Bridger Seward, the steward of the Knight's estates, and his family until he died in 1808. Jane Austen's mother was offered a choice of the house here or one in Kent by her son, Edward Austen (later Edward Knight). She chose this house and she and her daughters, Cassandra and Jane, moved here in 1809 after repairs had been made.

The house on the right is named Clinkers after the local blacksmiths who lived here. The gabled building on the left is the Grey Friar public house. On 7 January 1905, the *Hampshire Herald and Alton Gazette* announced that the Grey Friar at Chawton was to be taken over at end of month by the Hampshire Public House Trust. It was owned by the Knight family until put up for sale in 1951.

These cottages lie at the northern end of the village on the western side of the road to Alton. In the late 1800s, the post office was occupied by an Army pensioner called William Andrews who had married Annie Shilton, the post-mistress. Living nearby were a tailor, a bootmaker and a platelayer who must have worked on the local railway.

Eleven

Medstead
and Four Marks

PARISH CHURCH, MEDSTEAD.   VARNEY'S SERIES.

After the United Service to celebrate the Coronation of 1911, the church clock was unveiled by Miss Adelaide Gertrude Causton of Home Close, Medstead. There were said to be about 200 people present. Each child was presented with a medal at the children's tea and there was dancing in the evening after the adults had had their tea.

'As regards discipline the children are pleasantly behaved, frank and open . . . on the other hand they are talkative and mischievous in a careless and light-hearted way when their attention ought to be concentrated upon their lessons' reported one of His Majesty's inspectors when he visited Medstead School in 1914.

This view of Medstead School dates from before the alterations of 1926/27. Temporary classes were held in the village hall and the rectory barn. The foundation stone of the new part was laid on Friday 12 December 1926, and the school was officially re-opened on Empire Day (24 May) 1927.

116

In the 1870s, the smithy was run by the Westbrook family. By the time of the 1881 census, Dorset-born Thomas King had taken over as blacksmith. His son, Ernest, who was four years old at the time, was listed as the village blacksmith in a later directory of 1939.

Looking south down the High Street, the building on the right was Medstead post office. In 1895, Thomas King was blacksmith, cycle agent and ironmonger and sub-postmaster! After moving elsewhere in the village, the post office has now returned to its former home.

After the Second World War, Bessie and Albert Major renamed the smithy 'Crossways'. Bessie sold wool, baby linen, clothes, general drapery – 'nothing too small or too large'! Albert ran a television and radio business here and records could be ordered. Their adverts announced that they gave 'personal attention to all matters'.

The message on the back of this postcard reads 'he goes on Jan 15th, I think, unless its Feb 15th…come over to lunch one day and see the Rectory'. The card was signed by Maddie Swan and probably dates from 1922 – just before Revd Gerald Savoury came to Medstead. The Swans lived at Hattingley House.

The *Alton Gazette* of 24 June 1905, reported 'THE BAND! The Medstead Brass Band is still going strong, and is receiving a good deal of patronage. Three engagements last week and several more booked. Well done, the boys!' The first dance that winter took place in the band room in November, but there were only a few people present.

Before it was considerably altered in 1904/05, this was Manor Farm. In 1911, it was the home of Captain Edward Purefoy Ellis Jervoise RN, and a later owner was Lady Bradford. After the war it was acquired by an American Roman Catholic Order and the Convent of St Lucy was established.

This Congregational (later United Reform) chapel is in South Town Road, although it has been altered over the years. It opened on 14 August 1896 with an afternoon service, a public tea in Mr Gotelee's barn and an evening meeting. The total cost of the building was £196.

When Pullinger's Farm, Hattingley, was up for sale in 1911, the two houses on the left were included with it. One of them was said to be let, together with the garden, at a rent of £5 a year with the tenant paying the rates. The buildings were described as being of flint and brick with two rooms up and two down. The water supply was a good well at some nearby cottages.

Sent from Medstead in 1909, this card was addressed to Gretz in Seine et Marne, France. The premises were described as The Sanitorium and were run by the Broadlands Co. By 1920, Thomas Lloyd of West End Farm was secretary of the Broadlands Social Club.

In 1905, it was said that the village of Medstead had changed much during the past few years and that it would continue to do so. At that time, two large farms were being sold by Homesteads Ltd for small holdings and another farm had been sold by Messrs Marlow and Wright for the same purpose.

In the County Court of Hampshire holden at Alton.   L. 145

ELIZABETH RAKER, *Plaintiff,* v. ARTHUR RAKER, *Defendant.*

MEDSTEAD, HANTS.

About 1½ miles from Medstead Station on the L. & S.W. Railway.

Particulars and Conditions of Sale of

A CONVENIENTLY-ARRANGED

Freehold Bungalow

RESIDENCE,

KNOWN AS

'Hilly View,' Homestead Road,

TOGETHER WITH

About 4¾ acres of Meadow Land & Kitchen Garden,

Which

MR. CHARLES YOUNG

With the approbation of His Honour Judge GYE, the Judge of the County Court of Hampshire, pursuant to the Order in the said Action, dated 24th July, 1907, will SELL BY AUCTION,

AT

THE "SWAN HOTEL," ALTON,

On TUESDAY, OCTOBER 1st, 1907,

At SIX o'clock in the Afternoon, in One Lot.

Particulars and Conditions of Sale may be obtained at the Place of Sale, of MESSRS. BAILEY and WHITE, Solicitors, Winchester; or of the AUCTIONEER, Alton, Hants.

Mr W. Carter had disposed of Soldridge Farm in about 1902 and several houses had been erected on it. Builders were busy putting up villas, bungalows and cottages in and around the village of Medstead. The population rose by 44% in the twenty years between 1891 and 1911.

This station opened in 1868 and lay on the line between Alton and Winchester. Originally known as Medstead Station, it became Medstead and Four Marks Station in 1937. The last British Rail train passed through here 4 February 1973. The Mid-Hants Railway now runs trains between Alresford and Alton via this station.

In 1923, William Oates was living in Trinity House, Medstead, and he described himself as a charabanc proprietor. Six years later, William J. Oates was granted a petrol licence and, in 1933, he applied for permission to add to his premises in Four Marks. The Oates family are also remembered by local people as delivering wireless batteries in the van shown here.

In 1935, a request for a new petrol pump and tank and the removal of the other pump and tank to a new position at Chawton End Garage was agreed, subject to approval by the county council under the Restriction of Ribbon Development Act.

Post Office, Four Marks.

Posted in 1912, this view shows the premises of Mrs Mary Agnes Parsons, grocer and sub-postmistress. Four Marks was not a separate civil or ecclesiastical parish at this time and its post office was listed under the Ropley entry in the 1911 Hampshire Directory. As can be seen, good accommodation was also on offer here for passing cyclists. Sadly, this building has now been demolished.

Four Marks

The post office moved down Four Marks Hill, as it was known, and the new post mistress was K. Tomlinson. The Tomlinsons were also grocers and sold brand new British Army boots for 12s 6d a pair, agricultural boots for 10s 6d and pressure cured wellingtons for 19s 11d.

This picture of Winchester Road shows the crossing with Lymington Bottom Road before it was widened. The white building on the left was The Stores – home of Charles Campbell, shopkeeper. Hence this area became known as Campbell's Corner. Just after the war, the shop was advertised as 'The Four Marks Shopping Centre'.

In February 1959, Hampshire County Council proposed the provision of a twin carriageway between North Street, Ropley, and the top of Shant Hill at Four Marks. In May, general widening between Bishops Sutton and the Shant public house commenced. A year later work on the dual carriageway itself was started and, in February 1962, the scheme was reported to be complete.

Run by Marjorie Paxman, 'Priscillas' lay on the main Winchester Road. Deliveries of home-made cakes and jams were made to all parts of the area daily. Many other businesses – such as Arrow Stores, Campbells and Eddolls of Alresford – delivered at a time when most people did not own or have access to a car.

The church of the Good Shepherd, Four Marks, was consecrated by the Bishop of Winchester on Saturday 27 March 1954. Also attending the service were the rectors of Ovington, Itchen Abbas, Medstead, Farringdon, the vicar of Ropley, the rural dean of Alresford and the archdeacon of Basingstoke.

This nursery was in Brislands Lane and was one of several in the area. Fruit trees seem to have been in demand, costing 8s a dozen for four-year-old bushes. One business boasted of having forty kinds of apple tree to choose from, while there were thirty-eight varieties of roses from which to pick at 1s each – all dug while you waited.

On the left of this view lies the Mission Room, or Five Lanes End Church Room as it was also known. Made of corrugated iron, it still stands, although it is now covered with undergrowth. On the other side of the road is Belford House. Before the war, James Middleton Beck lived here. Having been recently extended, it is now a nursing home.

In 1895, the Alton Rural District Council recommended that The Telegraph be rented as a Sanitary Hospital because it was isolated and could be approached by good roads. The building, seen here, had been built as part of a line of semaphore towers between Plymouth and London. The line was never finished, being abandoned in 1831 due to the expense.